Understanding English Subject-Verb Agreement

A Guide to English as a Second Language for Teachers, Foreign English Learners, Adult Education, TOEFL, GRE, ESL Classes, and Homeschooling

TABLE OF CONTENTS

CHAPTER ONE

Introduction to Concord or Subject-Verb Agreement

Language is one of the most beautiful natural gifts you will ever find in the world. The way we speak and our choices of words all make language special. English language has a set of amazing rules and regulations. When you follow these rules, you will be able to convey your feelings and thoughts properly. Sometimes, after you tell someone else what you have in mind, you discover that you did not put it right. The problem may come from the lack of the knowledge of concord.

Concord in English is the agreement between the subject and the predicate. You must get these two things right to make a grammatically correct sentence. If the subject is wrong and the predicate is correct, the message will be confusing. If the subject is correct and the predicate is wrong, the entire sentence will still make no sense.

Now look at these sentences:

They is coming to my house today.

She are here.

They is our new neighbor.

We is late for work.

I are going to school/.

Albert and Alvin is brothers.

Sugar are sweet.

Imagine speaking or writing English that way. Your message will be confusing and no one will understand a single word you say. Every word you use may be correct but the way you combined those words can confuse people.

The knowledge of concord helps you use the right subject and the right verb together without causing confusion in meanings.

What is a Subject?

A subject is the name we give to the person or thing that performs the action in a sentence. A subject can be a noun or a pronoun. Do you still remember your lessons on nouns and pronouns? Nouns are names of persons, places, animals and things. Pronouns are words you use instead of nouns.

Examples of nouns

Andre	Oscar
Sandra	America
Philip	Canada
Jake	Australia

India   New York

Toronto   New   Delhi

Examples of pronouns

You   We

He   They

She   It

When you make them perform an action, they become subjects. For example:

1. **Andre** is a good person.
2. **Sandra** loves Andre.
3. **America** donated $20 million dollar to the United Nations.
4. **Canada** opened its borders to migrants.
5. **New Delhi** has beautiful sites.
6. **She** traveled to London last week.
7. **He** returned the missing item.

8. **We** changed the name of our company.
9. **You** saw the news this morning.
10. **I** trusted him but he disappointed me.

All the words written in bold are either nouns or pronouns. They are the subjects of the sentences. They perform the actions in those sentences. Action words are always verbs and they show what the subjects do, did or are doing.

Look at the same sentences once again. All the verbs are written in bold.

1. Andre **is** a good person.
2. Sandra **loves** Andre.
3. America **donated** $20 million dollar to the United Nations.
4. Canada **opened** its borders to migrants.
5. New Delhi **has** beautiful sites.

6. She **traveled** to London last week.
7. He **returned** the missing item.
8. We **changed** the name of our company.
9. You **saw** the news this morning.
10. I **trusted** him but he disappointed me.

What is a Predicate?

Predicates are verbs, and they may be main verbs or auxiliary verbs. Not all verbs show real actions. Some do not look like verbs but they still are. Some of the verbs that do not look like verbs are:

Is	Should
Are	Can
Has	Could
Have	Will
Shall	Would

The main or real verbs that show actions are:

Jump	Dig
Skip	Hit
Run	Open
Sit	Extend
See	Get
Look	Help
Meet	Invite
Fly	walk
Cry	yawn

Now let's put some of them in sentences

1. Mr. Steve **visits** his mother every weekend.
2. I **am** the owner of Jett Records.
3. Sarah **looks** sick.

4. Chuck **likes** ice cream.
5. The girls **think** they are the best jumpers.

The Rules of Concord

The general rule of concord simply states that:

i. A singular noun/pronoun takes a singular verb
ii. A plural noun/pronoun takes a plural verb

Singular nouns and pronouns

A singular noun or pronoun represents one person, one place or one thing.

Examples of singular nouns and pronouns are:

Jim (one person)

A table (one table)

Sarah (one person)

America (one country)

He (one person)

She (one person)

It (one thing)

New York (one city)

Plural nouns and pronouns

A plural noun or pronoun represents two or more persons, places or things.

Examples

Jim and Jake (two persons)

America and Canada (two countries)

Sarah and Mona (two persons)

You (acts as a plural pronoun)

We (plural pronoun)

They (plural pronoun)

Singular Verbs

A singular verb is a verb that represents the action performed by one person or one thing. Singular verbs go with singular subjects (singular nouns or singular pronouns.) Singular verbs often have the letter "s" at the end of the word. The letter "s" in singular verbs should not confuse you. The "s" does not make it a noun. Verbs function differently from nouns.

Examples of singular verbs are:

Jumps	Forgets
Kicks	Denies
Gives	Interprets
Looks	Calls
Thinks	Sits
Leaves	Stands
Visits	Makes
Forgives	Likes

Loves	Does
Bakes	Goes
Cooks	yawns

Plural Verbs

A plural verb is a verb that shows that more than one person is the performer of that verb or action. Plural verbs do not take the letter "s" at the end of the word.

Examples of Plural Verbs

Jump	Forgive
Kick	Forget
Give	Deny
Look	Interpret
Think	Call
Leave	Sit
Visit	Stand

Make	Cook
Like	Do
Love	Go
Bake	Yawn

Subject-Verb Agreement

When you write or speak, the verb you use must agree with the number of persons performing the action in the sentence. Use plural verbs with plural nouns or pronouns, and use singular verbs with singular nouns or pronouns. The rules of concord are easy, and you can master them in a short time. However, there are a few aspects you will need to study frequently to understand how they work and why they are written that way.

An example is **bread and butter.** Although they refer to two things, that is, "bread" and "butter", they are accepted as one item.

It is wrong to say "Bread and butter are my favorite meal."

But it is correct to say "Bread and butter is my favorite meal."

You can see why you need time and practice to master some aspects of concord. In the next chapters, we will discuss the rules of concord. Study them carefully and practice them regularly until you can construct grammatically correct sentences both in writing and in speech.

CHAPTER TWO

Concord Rule 1

When the subject in the sentence is in the singular, make the verb singular. This is because the number of persons in the sentence must correspond with the verb you use in the sentence.

Examples

1. **He sees** what happens.
2. **She knows** the best plan.
3. **The man tries** his best.
4. **The woman thinks** before she acts.
5. **The boy loves** ice cream.
6. **The girl chooses** for her parents.
7. **The dog climbs** the bed every time.
8. **The soldier fights** for his country.

9. **The woman looks** very beautiful.

10. **The doctor treats** a patient.

11. **The sailor knows** the way.

12. **The beggar lies** to people.

13. **He discovers** the truth every time.

14. **She remembers** the past always.

15. **A police officer protects** people.

16. **A judge listens** to lawsuits.

17. **He sleeps** on the streets.

18. **My sister studies** medicine.

19. **His brother wants** to live in the Maldives.

20. **My uncle drives** himself to work.

21. **The family doctor comes** over the weekend.

22. **The museum opens** at ten in the morning.

23. **The woman likes** jewelry.

24. **The school discourages** bullying and stealing.

25. **My father believes** in evolution.
26. **The game looks** interesting.
27. **The music sounds** cool.
28. **The cat is** cute and useful.
29. **A politician lives** in that mansion.
30. **A woman accuses** him of harassment.

Concord Rule 2

When you use **everyone**, **everything**, **everywhere**, or **everybody** in a sentence, use a singular verb, not plural verb. As long there is "every," the sentence will take the singular verb.

Examples

1. Everyone believes in something.
2. Everyone knows the truth about the president.

3. Everyone thinks to be special.
4. Everyone tells a lie at least once a day.
5. Everyone seeks to become rich.
6. Everyone laughs at very funny jokes.
7. Everyone likes pudding.
8. Everybody sees the truth.
9. Everybody means good to their loved ones.
10. Everybody fears guns and bullets.
11. Everybody screams when an accident happens.
12. Everybody is here unharmed.
13. Everybody hears the news flying around.
14. Everybody has one problem or another to solve.
15. Everything looks messy around here.
16. Everything makes sense now.
17. Everything makes me cry these days.

18. Everything sounds unreal to me.
19. Everything matches the suspects perfectly.
20. Everything is going to be fine.
21. Everything revolves around politicians.
22. Everywhere looks neat and tidy.
23. Everywhere is noisy nowadays.
24. Everywhere is good for me.
25. Everywhere looks the same to her.
26. Everywhere seems unsafe for people.
27. Everywhere is clean and airy.
28. Everywhere smells of flowers.
29. Everywhere makes me homesick.
30. Everywhere is my home and country.

Concord Rule 3

Use a plural verb for a prayer, wish, suggestion or recommendation even when the subject is singular.

Examples

1. I pray he heal fast. (not **I pray he heals fast**)
2. I pray the government listen to us.
3. I pray we leave this neighborhood next year.
4. I pray she love him as he loves her.
5. I pray my mother come home unharmed.
6. I pray my brother make it in life.
7. I wish God help him.
8. I wish he listen to me.
9. I wish my mother love me very much.
10. I wish the government create more jobs.
11. I hope his uncle come to his aid before it is too late.

12. I hope she understand how he feels.
13. I hope she get what she deserves.
14. I hope they find the missing boy.
15. I hope we win the match.
16. I suggest he look elsewhere.
17. I suggest she retrace her steps.
18. I suggest she think before she acts.
19. I suggest the woman find another man.
20. I suggest he stop bothering her for now.

Concord Rule 4

When the subject of the sentence contains a list of nouns or pronouns, the noun or pronoun closest to the verb, if they are separated by **or**, determines whether the verb will be singular or plural.

Examples

John, James or **I am** to blame. (correct)

In the sentence above, **I** is closest to the verb, that is why the right verb for the sentence is **am.**

John, James or I is to blame. (incorrect)

More examples

1. He, she or they are to take the prize.
2. He, you or I am not serious.
3. They, he or she has the key to the office.
4. His father, mother or sisters pay his rent.
5. The men, their wives or their friend is here.
6. The governors or the president loves this country.
7. The girl, her friends or boyfriend thinks he is smart.
8. My wife, my son and I love pudding.

9. He, she or the police officers are corrupt.

10. The author or writer is here.

CHAPTER THREE

Concord Rule 5

When a list of nouns or pronouns is linked with the connector "and," the verb will be plural.

Examples

1. They and I are friends.
2. She and he are going home.
3. The governor and the governors are here.
4. The man and his wife love this country.
5. The people and the president are the problem we have here.
6. My sister and her friend choose to ignore me.
7. His boss and the secretary are making plans to promote him.
8. The house and the garden are neat and clean.

9. The neighbors and their dogs
    are friendly.
10. The rivers and the villages are
    in the path of the volcano.

Concord Rule 6

When you start a sentence with **many a,** the verb must be singular, not plural.

Examples

1. Many a person volunteers to
    be vaccinated.
2. Many a boy loves football.
3. Many a girl is a good cook,
4. Many a dog is cute and
    friendly.
5. Many a book was on the floor.
    (not were on the floor)
6. Many a building has no
    electricity.
7. Many a man has good plans
    for family.

8. Many a government is confused and lacks direction.
9. Many a school knows what to do.
10. Many a student plans to join the navy.
11. Many a scientist supports the president.
12. Many a youth wants to get rich quick.'
13. Many a lawyer is dishonest and unreliable.
14. Many an applicant gets the job.
15. Many a candidate makes empty promises.
16. Many a machine breaks down in the night.
17. Many a friend becomes unfriendly when someone is in need.
18. Many a monkey likes bananas.
19. Many a religion teaches about God and love.
20. Many a dollar was lost in the production of vaccines.

Concord Rule 7

When you use **a pair of** in a sentence, the verb must be singular. Always use a singular verb for items that come in pairs.

Examples

1. A pair of trousers is all I need now.
2. A pair of binoculars is in my bag.
3. A pair of scissors lies on the floor over there.
4. A pair of eyes is enough for human beings.
5. A pair of chopsticks is in that store down the road.
6. A pair of jeans makes one look smart.
7. A pair of pants is part of the requirements.
8. A pair of shorts has its own use.
9. A pair of shoes is a necessity.

10. A pair of sandals complements shoes and sneakers.
11. A pair of gloves protects the hands.
12. A pair of handcuffs is hidden in the police officer's coat.

Concord Rule 8

When a collective noun stands for all members, use a plural verb. When a collective noun represents all the members as one body or one unit, use a singular verb.

Examples

1. The jury is not happy.
2. The jury are not happy.
3. Our club meets at 10 am.
4. Our club meet at 10 am.
5. The team is going to win.
6. The team are going to win.
7. My family plans to take a trip to Hawaii.

8. My family plan to take a trip to Hawaii.

CHAPTER FOUR

Concord Rule 9

When you provide extra information to the subject or subjects, the parenthetical statement you add should not change the choice of verb to use. Parenthetical statements are sentences that give additional information which does not make the sentence more or less meaningful. Commas often mark off parenthetical statements. These extra words are often introduced by "not."

Examples

1. The man, not his wife, comes here often.

2. The boy, not the girl, is here.
3. The father, not the children, cooks dinner.
4. The mayor, not the citizens, is honest.
5. The president, not the governors, knows what he is doing.
6. The captain, not the lieutenants, is strict and disciplined.
7. The king and queen, not their son, are intelligent.
8. The teachers, not the principal, make the school proud.
9. The managers, not their boss, are nice and humble.
10. The girl, not her parents, is smart.
11. The soldiers, not their commander, know the enemy's hideouts.
12. The ship, not the waves, is the problem.
13. The cats, not the dog, make loud noises.

14. The twin babies, not the teenage son, eat a lot of food.
15. The hotel owner, not the customers, needs reeducation.
16. The citizens, not the police, are to blame.
17. The building, not builders, needs reevaluation.
18. The man, not the woman, feels cold.
19. The mail carrier, not the taxi drivers, comes to this restaurant.
20. The monkeys, not the rabbit, run around the lab.

Concord Rule 10

When an additional group of words comes immediately after the subject or subjects, they must take the verb that corresponds with the number of persons the subject represents. These additional words are often introduced by **in addition to, together with, along with, alongside, like, with, no**

less than, **including**, or **in collaboration with**.

Examples

1. The president, together with his ministers, is here.
2. The men, together with a woman, have arrived.
3. The girl, together with her parents, sleeps in that building.
4. Our father, together with our uncles, loves football.
5. The citizen, together with the governors, met the president.
6. The lawyer, along with three state judges, is interested in the case.
7. The man, along with his children, thinks he is the smartest person in the world.
8. The sailors, along with the captain, lives on the ship.
9. The mangoes, along with the tree, are bad.

10. The women, along with the little girl, are against child marriage.
11. The teacher, with the students, loves mathematics.
12. The pilot, with her passengers, is excited.
13. The children, with their father, jump rope.
14. The man, no less than his children, is hungry.
15. The women, no less than their boss, are greedy.
16. The company, in collaboration with Disney and Marvel, is going places.
17. The cats, in addition to the dog, are a whole lot of work.
18. The movie, like its casts, is boring.
19. The food, as much as the drinks, looks cheap.
20. The cell phones, as much as the earpiece, are fake.

Concord Rule 11

When you use the words **more than** to begin a sentence, the verb in the sentence must correspond with the number closest to the verb.

Examples

More than one boy is here. (correct)

More than one boy are here. (wrong)

More than two boys are here. (correct)

More than three men come here every week. (correct)

More than three men comes here every week. (wrong)

More examples

1. More than two girls are present at the school party.
2. More than one boy is cleaning the room right now.

3. More than eight cars are at the parking lot.
4. More than three women prefer wage increase.
5. More than one motorbike breaks down every day.
6. More than three children play here.
7. More than one player is sick.
8. More than two pencils are in my bag.
9. More than five governors support the president.
10. More than ten birds die daily.
11. More than eleven bottles are broken.
12. More than one man is leaving the job.

Concord Rule 12

When you use indefinite pronouns, the verbs must be singular. Examples of indefinite pronouns are **everybody, everyone, everything, everywhere, nowhere, no one,**

**nobody, anywhere, anything, each,
nothing, something**, etc.

Examples

1. Everybody is fine and good.
2. Everybody sees who he is.
3. Everybody knows how to brush the teeth.
4. Everyone wants to know how the president is doing.
5. Everyone thinks the country is in a mess.
6. Nowhere is safe right now.
7. Nowhere seems clean enough for us to sit and have picnic.
8. No one wants to talk to us.
9. No one feels the way we do.
10. Anywhere is okay for me.
11. Anywhere looks the same to him.
12. Anything means nothing.
13. Anything causes allergies.
14. Each person knows his place.
15. Each orange is bad.
16. Each one has a virus.

17. Nothing is impossible if you have determination.
18. Nothing disturbs his peace of mind.
19. Nothing stops her from achieving her dreams.
20. Something is wrong somewhere.

CHAPTER FIVE

Concord Rule 13

When relative pronouns such as **whose, who, that** or **which** appears in a sentence, the verb must correspond with the subject or subjects these relative pronouns represent.

Examples

1. The **police officers** whose boss died **are** not going to resign.
2. The **women** whose businesses collapsed **need** government help.
3. The **man** whose children were murdered **is** now in London.
4. The **boy** whose parents disappeared last week **is** in foster care.

5. The **dogs** that ate the food **are** friendly.
6. The **cats** that stained the floor **are** cute.
7. The **shop owner** who threw shoes at people **is** in police custody.
8. The **baker** who poisoned the guests **is** nowhere to be found.
9. The **girls** who won the competition **are** from the same school.
10. The **apples**, which were spoiled, **are** in the waste bin.
11. The **boat**, which was built by a student, **is** on the sea.
12. The **sailors** who foresaw the storm **are** safe.

Concord Rule 14

Countable nouns take singular if they refer to one object. They take plural verbs if they refer to more than one object. Uncountable nouns do not have singular forms. They often act as one or a unit. Uncountable nouns take plural verbs.

Some of the things you can count are:

Chairs	Wristwatches
Tables	Shoes
Houses	Socks
Pens	Buckets
Pencils	Persons etc

Items or things that you cannot count because they are difficult or impossible to count are:

Flour	Sugar
Water	Butter
Sand	Luggage
Wind	Information
Air	Gas
Rice	Power

Money   Happiness

Love   Advice

1. The water splashes here and there.
2. The flour mixes with water.
3. The air is damp and wet.
4. The wind is stronger here than over there.
5. The man is coming.
6. The men are coming.
7. Ten persons were able to carry the boat.
8. One man was able to catch the thief.
9. Twenty tables were placed in
10. All the information he gives the police is inaccurate. (not were inaccurate)
11. All the advice my father gave my brother was helpful. (not **were helpful**)
12. Her huge luggage was easy to carry.
13. A lot of money was spent in the last elections.

14. Money is good, not bad.
15. A lot of sugar is in this tea.
16. Sugar is sweet; honey is sweeter.
17. Sand is used for building houses.
18. Milk is an ingredient for tea or coffee.
19. The chairs are good but the table is not.
20. The pencils look fine but the pen does not.

Concord Rule 15

Words that look like plurals because they have the letter "s" at the end go with singular verbs, not plural verbs.

Examples of these words are:

Mathematics

Statistics

Economics

Physics

Measles

Mumps

Tuberculosis

Shingles

Examples in sentences

1. Mathematics is a fun subject.
2. Physics is a science subject.
3. Economics is an important subject.
4. Statistics helps us to know the number of things involved in something.
5. Tuberculosis is a serious disease.
6. Civics makes one civil and patriotic.
7. Mumps covers every part of his body.
8. Measles is attacking children almost everywhere.

In addition, when you use words like **series**, **means**, **funds**, **goods**,

particulars, **wages**, etc, they must be followed by singular verbs.

Examples

1. The funds comes from the government. (funds here means money)
2. The series of events these days is alarming. (not are alarming)
3. The wages of the women has increased.
4. His goods was kept safe. (not were kept safe)
5. His particulars was incomplete. (not were incomplete)

Concord Rule 16

Use a plural verbs for two persons, two places or two objects joined by **and**.

Examples

1. The man and the woman are friends.
2. The boy and the girl were found.
3. The car and the truck collide here every time.
4. The cat and the dog play in the afternoon.
5. The table and the chair are new and strong.
6. The baby and her mother are alive and healthy.
7. The president and the governor come here every week.
8. The seller and the buyer have seen the new product.
9. The police and the victim's family know about the latest development.
10. The teacher and the student want new furniture.

However, there are situations when you have to take care not to confuse the subjects. Sometimes a subject can represent more than one person in sentence. Look at the following examples:

1. The president and chairperson is here. (correct)
2. The president and chairperson are here. (wrong)
3. The president and the chairperson is here. (wrong)
4. The president and the chairperson are here. (correct)

The first sentence refers to the same person. That is, the president is the same person as the chairperson. Therefore, the singular verb is what it uses.

The second sentence is wrong because the sentence means the same person, and you cannot use a plural verb when referring to one person.

How do you know when to use the singular or plural verb in sentences like these? It is simple. In sentence four and five, the examples show us that when there is no **the** before the titles, the sentence refers to the same person. But when there is **the**, the sentence refers to two different persons.

Examples

1. The teacher and author is here.

In the sentence above, the teacher is the same person as the author. That means the teacher is an author and he is the same person with the two titles. The omission of **the** is what helps you to know that the sentence means the same person.

2. The teacher and the author are here.

Here, the teacher is different from the author. They are not the same person. The use of **the** suggests that they are two entirely different persons.

CHAPTER SIX

Concord Rule 17

Noun phrases that refer to categories of people use plural verbs. Examples of these noun phrases are **the poor, the rich, the young, the helpless, the weak, the handicapped, the gifted, the young in spirit, the successful, the humble, the meek, the led, the leadership** etc.

Examples

1. The rich know not hunger or deprivations.
2. The poor suffer a lot in life.
3. The young know not what tomorrow holds.
4. The weak have no say in political matters.
5. The young in spirit have fresh ideas always.

6. The patient have a better future than others.
7. The wealthy think less of tomorrow.
8. The successful speak with pride.
9. The handicapped need help from healthy people.
10. The helpless often cry for help.
11. The gifted know what they have.
12. The leadership make the final decision for the company.

Concord Rule 18

Units of items, amount of money and length of objects take singular verbs. Examples of units, amounts and length are **one thousand, three thousand, ten million, twenty billion, one pound, two pounds, ten meters, twenty kilometers, five miles, fifty percent** etc.

Examples in sentences

1. Twenty minutes is not too long.
2. Ten hours of work is not bad.
3. Two pounds extra makes him happy.
4. Twenty miles is a long distance.
5. Sixty seconds makes one minute.
6. Sixty minutes makes one hours
7. Ten billion is a huge amount of money.
8. Twenty million was stolen from the vault.
9. Fifty percent is not fair.
10. Twenty kilometers is not enough to stop him.
11. Three thousand dollars is a huge amount these days.
12. Twelve meters between them is a turn off.

Concord Rule 19

When calculations are involved, use either the singular or the plural verb. Any one you use is correct, so do not worry.

Examples

1. One plus three is four. (correct)
2. One plus three are four. (correct)

More examples

1. Ten plus ten equals twenty.
2. Ten plus ten equal twenty.
3. Two plus two equals four.
4. Two plus two equal four.
5. Three plus four equals seven.
6. Three plus four equal seven.
7. Five plus one is six.
8. Five plus one are six.
9. Three minus two is one.
10. Four minus two are two.
11. Ten multiplied by three is thirty.

12. Ten multiplied by three are thirty.
13. Six multiplied by two is twelve.
14. Six multiplied by two are twelve.
15. Eight multiplied by three is twenty-four.
16. Eight multiplied by three are twenty-four.
17. Twelve divided by two is six.
18. Twelve divided by two are six.
19. Twenty divided by ten is two.
20. Twenty divided by ten are two.

Concord Rule 20

When a singular subject comes after **every**, it takes the singular verb.

Examples

1. Every man was asked to go home. (correct)

2. Every man were asked to go home. (wrong)
3. Every girl is present here. (correct)
4. Every girl are present here. (wrong)

More examples

1. Every person speaks his mind.
2. Every girl knows the truth.
3. Every boy sees the need for education.
4. Every parent needs money.
5. Every soldier has a gun.
6. Every sailor knows about shipping.
7. Every president loves the country.
8. Every mother cares for children.
9. Every father thinks about more money.
10. Every student goes to school.

When **and** joins two subjects, use the singular verb too.

Examples

1. Every man and woman loves the country.
2. Every boy and girls goes to school.
3. Every night and day brings fear.
4. Every cat and dog runs away when the fox comes.
5. Every teacher and student loves to learn.
6. Every father and mother cares for children.
7. Every soldier and civilian obeys the law.
8. Every boss and employee is honest and kind.
9. Every day and week brings joy.
10. Every child and teenager is healthy and strong.

CHAPTER SEVEN

Concord Rule 21

When the word **most** starts a sentence, the verb will depend on the number of the subject. If the subject is singular, the verb will be singular. If the subject is plural, the verb will be plural. It also is dependent on whether the subject is a countable or an uncountable noun.

Examples

1. Most of the boys are in school.
2. Most of the girls are at home with their mothers.
3. Most of the fathers are working on the farms.
4. Most of the engineers are on the bridge
5. Most of the students are coming home.

6. Most of the food is gone.
    (uncountable noun)
7. Most of the water has leaked
    away.
8. Most of the time is gone.
9. Most of the staff has resigned.
10. Most of the flour is needed for
    the dough.
11. Most of the sugar is on the
    floor.
12. Most of the sand is in the box.
13. Most of the air has escaped.
14. Most of the wind blows here.
15. Most of the fire burns there.

The same rule applies when you use
much to begin a sentence.

Examples

1. Much of the water has leaked
    out.
2. Much of the food is gone.
3. Much of the milk is spilled.

Concord Rule 22

When **all** appears at the beginning of a sentence, the verb will depend on the meaning of **all** in that sentence. Sometimes **all** may mean **everyone** or **everything**. Other times, **all** may mean **all the things** or **all the people involved**. If **all** means **everyone** or **everything**, use a singular verb. If it means **all things** or **all the people involved**, use a plural verb.

Look at these examples

1. **All is** going to be all right.
2. **All is** well with us.
3. **All** he said **is** wrong.
4. **All is** looking good financially.
5. **All is** well with her for now.
6. **All** the people **are** coming.
7. **All** the men **were** there.
8. **All** the boys **are** good.
9. **All** the bottles **are** broken.
10. **All** the students **run** for the high school.

When **all but** is involved, the verb should be plural, not singular.

Examples

1. **All** but Kim **were** at the party.
2. **All** but John **come** here every day.
3. **All** but the boy **love** football.
4. **All** but Joan **think** otherwise.
5. **All** but the president **are** honest.

Concord Rule 23

The use of **either or** and **neither nor** can get students confused. Nevertheless, it is something every learner can master if they study concord carefully. The rule is simple: if **either or** or **neither nor** joins two singular subjects, the sentence takes a singular verb. If **either or** or **neither nor** joins a singular subject and a plural subject, the subject closer the verb determines the form of verb to use.

Examples

1. Either John or James is the owner of that bag.
2. Either Joan or Kim **comes** here.
3. Either my mother or my father **is** responsible.
4. Either my friend or my brother **knows** about this matter.
5. Either my wife or my kid **is** in trouble.
6. Neither the president nor the governor **thinks** of the future.

7. Neither the man nor the woman **knows** what happened.
8. Neither the cat nor the dog **eats** at midnight.
9. Neither the pot nor the plate **was** in the right place.
10. Neither the teacher nor the student **knows** the answer.

Look at another example

1. Either the boy or the girls **understand** the value of education.
2. Either the girls or the boy **understands** the value of education.
3. Either the mechanic or the drivers **see** the fault.
4. Either the drivers or the mechanic **sees** the fault.

Use the same rule when writing sentences that involve **not only but also**.

Examples

1. Not only Sam but also even Sarah **loves** movies.
2. Not only Sam but also the girls **love** movies.
3. Not only the girls but also even Sam **loves** movies.
4. Not only the president but also the governors **hate** bribery and corruption.
5. Not only the governors but also the president **hates** bribery and corruption.

Concord Rule 24

When **each one** or **one of** comes at the beginning of a sentence, the verb must be singular.

Examples

1. Each one of the boys is in the hall.
2. Each one of the balls is in the box.

3. Each one of the animals drinks water in the pond.
4. Each one of the women has seen the mayor.
5. Each one of the girls has a bright future.
6. One of the girls is feeling unwell.
7. One of the soldiers comes here.
8. One of the beggars knows the shop owner.
9. One of the students loves mathematics.
10. One of the birds perches on that tree over there.

Sometimes, the sentence will come in the form of **she is one of** or **he is one of**. This type of sentence construction is different and often takes a plural verb.

Examples

1. She is one of the girls who run for the school.

2. He is one of the boys who work at the post office.

CHAPTER EIGHT

Practice Test Questions on Concord/Subject-Verb Agreement

Fill the gap in the sentence with the correct verb

1. He and I _______ friends.
   A. Am   B. is   C. are

2. Each of the men _______ present at the party.
   A. Are   B. is   C. were

3. Neither you or she _______ to blame.
   A. Is   B. are   C. am

4. The aim of the seminars _______ to educate the people.
   A. Are   B. is   C. am

5. Three and seven _______ ten.

A. Making   B. made   C. makes

6. Mathematics _____ an interesting subject.

A. Is   B. are   C. were

7. Two hundred miles _____ too long.

A. Are   B. is

8. Fifty dollar _____ a huge amount of money.

A. Are   B. is

9. Either they or he _____ is the problem.

A. Are   B. is   C. am

10. James as well as his parents _____ well behaved.

A. Are   B. is

11. Is it he who _____ at the door.

A. Am   B. are   C. is

12. Bread and butter _____ my favorite meal.

A. Are   B. is

13. The man and the woman ______ to see you.

A. Want   B. wants

14. The captain and the author ______ here.

A. Are   B. is

15. The student and musician ______ football too.

A. Loves   B. love

16. One of his friends ______ come.

A. Have   B. has

17. Every boy and every girl ______ the president.

A. Adores   B. adore

18. She is one of the women who ______ the news.

A. Reads   B. read

19. My father, along with my sisters, ______ in this house.

A. Live   B. lives

20. One of the senior workers ______ unwell.

A. Look   B. looks

21. Kim, along with her sisters, ______ learnt their lesson.

A. Have   B. has

22. My friend as well as my brother _____ college.

A. Attend   B. attends

23. She and I _____ finished the work.

A. Have   B. has   C. am

24. Either he or I _____ to receive to prize.

a. Am   B. is   C. are

25. Politics _____ is game and nothing more.

A. Are   B. is

26. The news about the accident _____ a sad one.

A. Is   B. are

27. A good deal of issues _____avoided by the committee.

A. Was   B. were

28. The result of the medical test _____ not yet out.

A. Is   B. are

29. Driving _____ fun.

A. Is   B. are

30. Knowledge of concord ____ important.

A. Is   B. are

31. His only source of income _____ teaching.

A. Was   B. were

32. The ideas of my brother _____ from mine.

A. Differs   B. differ

33. There ____ many who think the world will end someday.

A. Is   B. are

34. The cost of fuel, food and clothing ____ high.

A. Is   B. are

35. John and I _____ friends.

A. Is   B. am   C. are

36. Tim and Kim ____ coming.

A. Is   B. are

37. Neither Jake nor Kara ____ about the incident.

A. Knows   B. know

38. Neither you nor I ____ to take her to the hospital.

A. Is   B. are   C. am

39. Either he or I _____ to see him now.

A. Is   B. am   C. are

40. Neither their father nor their children _____ arrived.

a. Has   B. have

41. Each boy and each girl _____ a red bag.

A. Has   B. have

42. Not only the man but his sisters _____ everything.

A. Knows   B. know

43. Neither the players nor the coach _____ happy.

A. Is   B. are

44. Either Francis or you _____ not serious.

A. Is   B. are

45. The car with its tires _____ burnt.

A. Was   B. were

46. The teacher and artist _____ here.

A. Live   B. lives

47. The lawyer and the poet _____ music.

a. Love   B. loves

48. The tall man, together with his beautiful wife, _____ to meet the manager.

a. Want   B. wants

49. The sailors, along with their captain, _____ sick.

A. Is   B. are

50. The boy not his father _____ pudding.

A. Likes   B. like

ANSWERS TO PRACTICE TEST QUESTIONS

1. Are	26. Is
2. Is	27. Was
3. Is	28. Is
4. Is	29. Is
5. Make	30. Is
6. Is	31. Was
7. Is	32. Differ
8. Is	33. Are
9. Is	34. Is
10. Is	35. Are
11. Is	36. Are
12. Is	37. Knows
13. Want	38. Am
14. Are	39. Am
15. Loves	40. Have
16. Has	41. Has
17. Adores	42. Knows
18. Read	43. Is
19. Lives	44. Are
20. Looks	45. Was
21. Has	46. Lives
22. Attends	47. Love
23. Have	48. Wants
24. Am	49. Are
25. Is	50. likes

About the Publisher

Goodman Publishing is a company dedicated to producing books on English Language, General Studies, Teaching Practice, and the development and learning of listening, writing, reading and speaking skills.

With the help of our professional, trained and experienced staff and contributors, we strive to give our readers the best of experiences.

We understand the importance of the English Language and the reality that the world is fast becoming a global village, thanks to technology. We make our books as simple and understandable as possible so that learners of English will find each topic and volume easy to learn and master.

We publish a new book every month.

Goodman Publishing

Books by the Same Publisher